island, name

translated from the Finnish

saari, nimetön luoto

Martti Hynynen

by

MIKE HORWOOD

Published by Cinnamon Press
Meirion House
Glan yr afon
Tanygrisiau
Blaenau Ffestiniog
Gwynedd
LL41 3SU
www.cinnamonpress.com

ISBN: 978-1-905614-91-2

British Library Cataloguing in Publication Data. A CIP record for this book can be obtained from the British Library.

Designed and typeset in Palatino by Cinnamon Press. Cover design by Mike Fortune-Wood from original artwork 'silence on the sea of silence' by Olga Kharitonova; agency: dreamstime.com.
Printed by the MPG Books Group

Acknowledgements:

Thanks to Werner Söderström OY, who originally published saari, nimetön luoto in Finnish in 1991.

Acknowledgements are due to the editors of the following publications, in which some of these translations first appeared: *Modern Poetry In Translation, Envoi, Poetry Ireland Review.*

It is a great pleasure to express my thanks to Martti Hynynen for his valuable comments on the translations and his interest in the whole project. I am indebted to Eevi Apponen for assistance with many aspects of Finnish usage.

Contents

Introduction to *island, nameless rock*

Martti Hynynen was born in Rovaniemi, Finland, close to the Arctic Circle, in 1952 and grew up on the banks of Kemijoki, Finland´s largest river. His first collection, saari, nimetön luoto (island, nameless rock) was published by Werner Söderström in 1991. My aim when translating these poems has been to remain as faithful to the content and meaning of the original poems as possible. In the current debate in poetry translation between literal equivalence or versions, I have favoured the former approach in this case. Of course, literal translation is an unreachable ideal that is beset with inevitable difficulties and the need to compromise but it is the ideal that I kept before me.

Most of Martti Hynynen´s poems contain fairly simple and straightforward diction. However, the content is often neither simple nor straightforward. The images, situations and events are often surreal and although the diction is simple, the syntax is sometimes unconventional. Furthermore, he employs a pared back, minimalist style, focusing only on the critical details of an event and leaving out all explanatory or scene-setting information. In a comment on the absence of capital letters at the start of most of the poems, Hynynen has also revealed something of his working method and provided an explanation of his minimalist style:

One explanation for not using capital letters is that the poem has already started earlier, I just hurry to write down as the story goes on. They should be like imprints of my mind with no beginning and no end.

The tone of the poems in this collection is tentative and unassuming, the imagery is typically modest and humble;

potatoes and snails, for example, feature in several poems. This is partly the result of the simple diction already mentioned but the use Hynynen makes of simple words is often not simple. Hynynen has said that he likes to use simple words in unexpected places and it is partly this technique that creates the surreal quality that many of his poems possess. A good example of this method is the poem, `My Vernal Ecstasy´, where the vision of hot-air ballooning snails is both surprising and delightful. The reader might wonder where the idea comes from. Martti Hynynen has explained that he had heard that the French refer to a glass of cheap red wine as `a red balloon´ and he took the phrase and used it literally. The image thus works at two levels, the snails are being eaten at dinner and washed down with red wine and they are also enjoying a trip to the seaside by hot-air balloon. The image is wonderfully comic as well as surreal, of course, and the Finnish language allows for a further refinement. The word that I have translated as `well-done´ is `kypsät´ in Finnish and it has two meanings, `well-done´ in the cooking sense and `mature´ in the growing up sense. So these snails are not youngsters. And that, I have to say, is a truly wonderful concept. Alas, English wouldn´t allow me to bring in the second meaning.

In addition to some meanings that cannot be rendered into English, there are also a few cultural elements in one or two of the poems that it might be useful to know about. In the opening poem, the rocks that border the field are a familiar feature of the Finnish countryside. They come to be there as a result of the land being cleared for farming in earlier centuries, an especially back-breaking task in those days. They are emblematic of the old rural way of life and traditions of Finnish culture and in the poem form a link with that lifestyle. In `Appraisal Of The Collection´, the reference to `our brother nation´ would suggest Estonia most strongly to Finnish readers. The poem was written before Estonia gained independence and was still occupied by Russia. It is easy, then, to understand why these snails learn to recognize the danger posed by the middle-aged nature study group, an image of Russia. The `shrill-voiced´ leader is a wonderful comic touch.

Hynynen´s poems are wonderfully comic, but in many, such as `Appraisal´, there is an atmosphere of threat and danger. This is often suggested, or just off-stage. Consider `Dispersion´, for instance, with its barricades, curfew and children standing in the middle of a desert. Survival depends on having the wisdom to take evasive action, like the snails, or the ability to blend in with the background and escape notice, a practice that is reflected in the modest and unassuming quality of Hynynen´s language. Yet despite the dark tone of many of these poems, the emphasis is on surviving and on enjoying the humour that the ironic observing eye identifies.

Mike Horwood

island, nameless rock

saari, nimetön luoto

`I was born....'

I was born
when someone held a mirror
to my mouth,

my breath
still clouds it, but at that time
the wind came from the north

over white
fields, bordered with
rocks like heavy

jewels

Weariness In The Afternoon

Judgement day is already past.
The bassoon players are talking in undertones
while packing their instruments.

A crowd of strangers
rises from the graves.
Somewhere a great iron gate is welded shut.

A goblet of water
is brought to me
from a spring that flows into the garden.

The servant's eyes, bloodshot from the smoke,
flicker in the tray's
newly polished surface.

Safety Measures

having done what
they expected of me
I leave my statue on the balcony

to wave to the subdued
crowds and go
by way of the short corridor and staircase

into the cellar, where a tunnel
gently slopes down to a long central hall

from which eight
or nine routes branch
back to the earth's surface;

I choose one of them
and in a short while
emerge into the air

hearing the empty flagpole cords
flap along the darkening
edge of the town square

Dis-Connections

in the evening
when someone lifts me
to their ear

and expects to hear
the sea's roar
or perhaps the wind

woven with the sirens'
song, they get
the sound of

creaking oars
rhythmic drumming
and the lazy lashing of the whip on the rowers' backs

Dawn

Waiting for the Great Victor
we've already heard the drumming
of hooves

and noticed the dust cloud
far away over the plain; we have
still a little time

a moment —

maybe they will stay overnight,
build their campfire at the river's edge
continue their journey only at dawn —

I don't know my sister,
I don't know my brother,
but this is
the only life I know

Tuesday Is A Great Day

At the weekend the men could leave
for a while the felling of trees

that will eventually be made into telegraph poles
and lampposts that will stretch across

the countryside. The work rate only
gets back to its peak by Tuesday

when the world is built with
few words even though all the earlier

difficulties remain. Suddenly from the dark
sky the drizzling rain seems appropriate,

as does the report in the news
of the troops' concentration on the future battlefield.

Appraisal Of The Collection

during the crutch collection on behalf
of our brother nation, and before the final result

proved it to have been the most successful ever,
I considered how snails, sovereigns of the world,

wise and liberated, free-thinkers
with a broad concept of reality

learn when still young the most important things;
the alphabet of the rain dance, and to recognise

from the earth's quaking how danger threatens
when the middle-aged group are taken outdoors

to learn under shrill-voiced guidance
how to identify various species of bush

Dispersion

The framework of the children's sandbox
was used

as reinforcement
for the street barricade, so that

since the beginning of the week, after
the lifting of the curfew

the tired customers
have been standing

with blue spades
in their hands in the middle

of a desert.

Chances Of Success

perhaps you see
me as one in a procession:
my right hand of glass,
my left hand of iron
my arms clasped round the mirror's frame,
which rises high above my head
and is carried with ease as far as
it is only possible

though even at the start of the parade
it is often necessary to go back
and take replacements for those that have fallen

Frame

on the journey home
after the mushroom exhibition

with the taste of compost
in my mouth

I gave way to the radiation safety
centre's jeep

on the paving
in front of the library

Reconciliation

my white god
and my green

god
stretch out their hands

to each other, and make a bridge
on which I pause

before their broad
kind gaze

To Be Remembered When Dressing

It makes sense
to put on your disguise

in several layers;
for during your journey

you have to strip off
one layer after another

finally there is only
a shivering shadow on the road

that the rain hits
until the night takes even this

with it

Practice

only masters
are able to stand

in front of the unpainted
woodshed still

and alert
always ready

to blend in
with their background

Happiness On The Open Sea

on the blue sea
the singing slaves
row

on the blue sea
the rowing slaves
sing

light in the hand
grows
the oar

sweet
on the ear
the music

strange
the distant
shore

Dropping Out

just when nothing
should go

wrong, when I'm trying
to live as modestly

as possible, a car
stops on the road and the couple

stretching their legs ask
in passing if the place

is up for sale

Quietness

on the same morning
that I built a throne

from wood and stone
between the pines

the grass whispered:
why be content

to spend your whole life
in this unknown country

Boulevard

it was the time
of year when

you could still count
the yellow leaves

on the grass
in the park

transient

though it sometimes
still comes back to you

like your old
address

State Of Readiness

this is how it ought to be
            when the first patches of earth

appear in melting snow; we are ready
at the foot of the Reconstruction Memorial

our moment in the sun
                                    invincible
                                    before
the lonely railway carriages

A Brief Observation

after the seriousness
of birth has diminished

the end is getting closer
and this life

is heaven

The Small Print

when you speak your mind
when you appeal to fair play

when you go by the book
when you start a new life

when you go about thoughtfully
when you smile at yourself

when you draw conclusions
when you keep track of your time

when you refuse to sidestep
the blow
strikes home

Seeking Expression

between chewing
seldom smile

between chewing
seldom smile

between chewing
seldom smile

and
between chewing

it's almost become
speech

Are You Sure

        on that August evening
which you remember because you'd noticed
the sunset for the first time

        the sun's last proud glow
in the Scots pines on top of the hill
what happened
        on that August evening

when with misty eyes you turned back
towards your house
are you sure that your bare feet didn't
        sink through the lawn

        groping for the bedrock

Heard While Travelling

Were they the blows
of the hammer

as the chisel was searching
for the form hidden

in stone, or the irregular
beats of my own

heart
as the pursuers′ torches

were drawing away
to be engulfed

in the long, lucky night

Tactical Operations

learn to walk, learn to talk
retreat from the womb into hysteria

don't mark your route
don't speak with the lost

Credo

with lengthy strides
over the graves

meditating the significance
of those fat envelopes

Hindsight

the fortunate among us
find their own
Siberia –

the rest of us stay
here, and have to sing
all night

Pictures In My Palm

at rest inside me there are
extinct volcanoes on the seabed

warriors leaning
on their spears, I feel

the burn in the bell-ringers′
chafed palms

and the moon rising
over the darkened town

An Imaginary Dialogue Between Mihaly Vörösmartyn and John Donne

V: Now is winter and cold and snow and death.
D: Send me some honey to make sweet my hive.

A Humble Observation

at the interment
of those thirty potatoes

there should have been
a majestic bird

crossing the heavens
forging its way north

which could later
have been interpreted

as a lucky omen

Sky Beckons, Earth Beckons

it's getting late
the sky's getting lower

forcing me to stoop until
my legs give way

and night's black grass
enters my mouth

Crack

as land's and sea's perfection is broken
            on the shore, the night
draws in with flaming sails against your breast

Profane Days

you put questions to me
so we walk back to the garden

settle ourselves down like seeds in an apple
that a hand reaches towards, then hesitates

Clarity

years pass then something brings that time
back to me, it's just as well that you can't

remember anything specific
– or if you recall exactly what I once

said, you immediately suspect it was someone else
sitting opposite you at the same table

who said it, only yesterday

Assignments

It's August, the embers are still glowing.

Tomorrow you leave for the island
to collect potent herbs,

I will stay here carving
more arrowheads from bone.

The glacier will slip closer.

Message

                                                  that
there's an island, a nameless rock
   in international waters, which
         is not even marked on old sea charts:

a resting place for wood pigeons and yellow thrushes
   whose meetings late in the evening in thick grass
         escaped the artist's eye

so that the cliff face was engraved
   with a swan-necked boat and two figures
         so far apart from each other

                                                  that
anybody, anywhere
   would understand the meaning
         of longing

Change Of Season

In this corner of the universe
autumn begins tomorrow. Today is

mixing colours and making a brush
from the hair of the pine marten caught in spring

and then in the morning shifting
a few old pictures from my mind onto the cave's walls.

Remember

I loved you
like the leaves which

autumn writes about:
my life flashing
in pictures

through your
fingers

Requiem

allow
me to stare

these eyes that look
on other times
are all I have

these are evil days
snow and darkness
cover the tracks

as frost tightens its grip, the forest sighs;
nil inultum remanebit

Connection

between us an ocean
desert

the forest has grown
into masts

I want

to send my birds
to soar

without resting, without singing
until, sleepless, they reach

your shores

Us

the sea in one palm, earth in the other
I look for you to say goodbye

like the shore saying goodbye to the waves
over and over again

always with open arms

Meeting

like black and white
meeting and becoming colourful

triangles even as we watch
tables disappearing into space

and you are happy and restless
chosen by the same power

my osmotic sister

Migration

at the very first stirring
my airtight, upright

sarcophagus breaks
into pieces,

each fragment
starting to turn green

even as it falls
and the seeds

sink into clay
coming up as small trees

and clumps of grass
ready to take root

in the cracks between
the town square's paving

Events

sand and the undertow:
they move

the pebbles
that the shore had arranged

In Time

the frozen
bulrushes rustle
for the last time

the waves
rub footprints
into the beach's memory

Sideways

where I stood in summer
in the company of flies

and bumble bees
beside a table carried into a meadow

there is now a space
the same shape as me,

on the silent table
a snowy cloth

Revelation

The stone will be rolled away from the earth cellar's entrance
and we'll fall to the ground

hands reaching towards the sky
each in our own way

even though we lack
the natural wisdom of the sacred

potato shoots

My Vernal Ecstasy

new grass waves in the ether
attractively

a vision catches
the eye:

well-done snails carried
by red balloons

make their journey
towards the sea

Growing Season

leave the black
coat on the hook

shoots begin to sprout
from the potato, many

heavy cares
pass through

the lucid mind

A Lingering Look

as the snows disappear
into the forest

the shivering of your hands
is the longing

in wing beats
in a moonless

sky, a solitary
flight

towards your own
light

Recurring Signs

many springs drift
under the bridges

these women
shouldn't they be dressed
in leaves

striking your eye
like a garage
                door

Foundry Worker

if I’d had the choice
I would have liked to have been

the bell that men listen to
while eating their lunch

under a tree, the chimes
echoing into the distance and

dying away, they get up
take their backpacks and caps

and leave

Elements

when the words
were still unspoken

I didn't know
how

sad
the stone is

how grateful
the wild

grass

Further Information

Among a group
of lonely Brazilians

in the hospital canteen
I am realistic

and trust my bearings,
having successfully

negotiated the terrifying
symmetry of unraked paths

The Background

The removals lorry didn't
turn up and the group

quickly dispersed
without further instructions

dismantling several
tables in silence

and the scaffolding
that had supported

decisions made
in a carefree moment

For The Third Time

All the station masters in me
with their bright caps

(whose closed-down workplaces
were put up for auction years ago

along with the outbuildings
and stone cellars

leaving the amicable rivals
to discuss at leisure

after the event
how to interpret

the transference clause
though without arriving

at anything definite
regarding commencement

of the demolition work)
are still waving

their green flags and saluting
as the trains whistle past.

On The Steps In Fine Rain

as I was taking the rake
to the shed

it began to rain
I stood on the steps

for a long time with my hand
on the door knob

staring at the point in the darkening sky
where comet Wirtanen

was first observed
in 1948

Repair

the years pile up
their produce

this summer it's
the same, the roof-mender

drops in
a decent man

business is
business

no worries
let the grass grow

Important Excavation

on a spring morning
the snows melted from south-facing slopes
I call
my grey fox

and it comes from the forest
hesitantly,
digs open
my shallow grave beside the ridge

letting
my rested soul
continue its journey between the pines
down to the brook
and along its bank

The Structure Of An Answer

how do you explain
to those who have always lived in the sun
the meaning of night

                                        you will need
to use all your fingers if you're to do it
the nails scratching sensibly
                                        on the wall

Decision

we cannot see
ourselves
and nobody sees us

we are not
boats lying at anchor
as the sun dissolves into mist

when the right wave strikes
it drives us onto the open sea

Observation I: 15.07.1990

without learning anything
properly

you learn
to be your own

secretly drafted
arbitration proposal:

a useless, genuine
agreement

with no
signature

Mistakes

It was not spring
        with newly-grown grass
or fluffy moss creeping
        up the hanged man's leg to the fir tree,

it was the green glass of a smashed bottle
        along the top of the wall round the garden
to which the gate or secret door
        could not be found

Commonplace Advice

A few dark
shadows are enough

friend, those who
remember

will believe in former
innocence

Martti Hynynen was born in Rovaniemi, Finland, close to the Arctic Circle, in 1952 and grew up on the banks of Kemijoki, Finland´s greatest river. His first collection, *saari, nimetön luoto (island, nameless rock)*, was published in 1991 by Werner Söderström. Martti now lives in Tampere in the south of Finland where he works for the broadcasting company YLE.

Mike Horwood was born in London in 1955. He has lived in Greece and Switzerland and now lives in Finland where he teaches English to adult students. Mike has recently completed an online M.A. in creative writing at Manchester Metropolitan University and his poems have appeared in many magazines and anthologies.